D0577627

Energy at Work

Fossil Fuel Power

by Josepha Sherman

Consultant:
Steve Brick
Associate Director
Energy Center of Wisconsin
Madison, Wisconsin

Capstone
press

Mankato, Minnesota

Fact Finders is published by Capstone Press
151 Good Counsel Drive, P.O. Box 669, Mankato, Minnesota 56002
http://www.capstonepress.com

Library of Congress Cataloging-in-Publication Data
Sherman, Josepha.
    Fossil fuel power / by Josepha Sherman.
    p. cm.—(Fact finders. Energy at work)
    Summary: Introduces the history, uses, production, advantages and disadvantages,
and future of fossil fuel energy as a power resource.
    Includes bibliographical references and index.
    ISBN 0-7368-2470-7 (hardcover)
    1. Fossil fuels—Juvenile literature. [1. Fossil fuels.] I. Title. II. Series.
TP318.3.S44 2004
333.8'2—dc22   2003012915

Editorial Credits
Christopher Harbo, editor; Juliette Peters, designer; Alta Schaffer, photo researcher;
    Eric Kudalis, product planning editor

Photo Credits
Cover: Silhouette of an oil well, Index Stock Imagery/Ewing Galloway

Corbis/Bettmann, 13, 15; Corbis/Jonathan Blair, 16–17; Corbis/Royalty Free, 1, 9, 24–25;
Corbis/Tim Wright, 6–7; David R. Frazier Photolibrary, 4–5, 18, 22; Hulton/Archive by
Getty Images, 12, 14; Image courtesy Syncrude Canada Ltd., 8; The Image Finders/Howard
Ande, 23; Library of Congress, 10–11; NREL/Andrew Carlin-Tracy Operators, 26;
PhotoDisc Inc., 27; Thomas Kitchin/Tom Stack & Associates, 20–21

1 2 3 4 5 6 09 08 07 06 05 04

Table of Contents

Chapter 1

Kingston Power

Two smokestacks stand as tall as skyscrapers on the banks of the Tennessee River. They look like giants guarding the Kingston Power Plant.

Kingston is a coal-fired power plant. Every day, a train pulling more than 100 railroad cars brings coal to the plant. Most of the coal comes from Kentucky, Virginia, West Virginia, and Tennessee. After it is dumped, the coal is ground as fine as powder. It is then burned to make electricity. The Kingston Power Plant makes enough electricity to serve 1 million homes each year.

A long line of railroad cars carries coal to the Kingston Power Plant in Tennessee.

5

Chapter 2

Fossil Fuels

Coal, petroleum, and natural gas are called **fossil** fuels. A fossil is a plant or animal that died millions of years ago that hardened as rock. Fossils and fossil fuels are made when layers of soil press down on dead plants and animals. It takes millions of years for fossils and fossil fuels to be made.

Coal

The world has more coal than any other fossil fuel. This solid, black material is mined from the ground. Once mined, coal is usually burned for heat or to make electricity.

Coal is a solid fossil fuel that looks like black rock.

Coal is mined all over the world. The United States has 25 percent of the world's coal. Much of it is mined in Pennsylvania, West Virginia, Montana, and Wyoming. China, Russia, and India also mine coal.

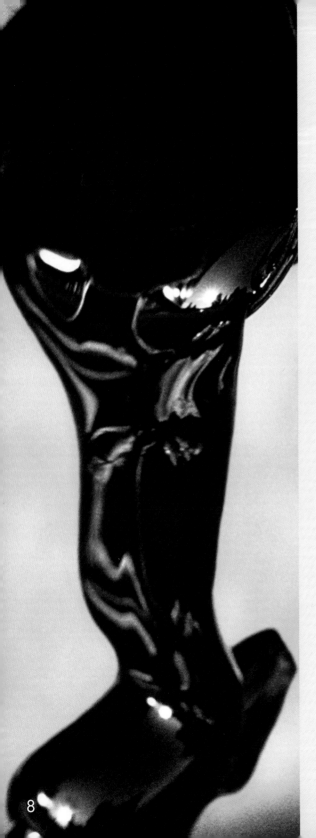

Petroleum

Petroleum, or oil, is a thick, black liquid. It is often made into home heating oil and gasoline. Petroleum is also used to make plastics and chemicals.

In the United States, most oil is used as fuel for cars, trucks, and airplanes. Most oil drilled in the United States comes from Texas, Alaska, and California.

Almost all of the world's oil is drilled in the Middle East. Saudi Arabia, Iran, Iraq, and Kuwait drill most of the oil in the Middle East.

Crude oil is a thick, black liquid.

Natural Gas

Natural gas is a colorless, odorless gas. It is used for heating, cooking, and making electricity.

Natural gas wells are often drilled near oil supplies. About 70 percent of the world's natural gas is found in the Middle East and Central Asia. Most of the United States' natural gas is drilled in Louisiana and Texas.

▲ Natural gas releases less pollution than other fossil fuels when it burns.

FACT!

Natural gas has no odor. A rotten egg smell is added to natural gas. The odor helps people smell a gas leak.

Chapter 3

Fossil Fuel History

Fossil fuels have been used for thousands of years. In about 500 B.C., the Chinese piped natural gas from wells using bamboo pipes. They burned natural gas to boil salt from seawater to make it drinkable. American Indians in the eastern United States made paint and medicines with petroleum. For hundreds of years, people burned coal to heat metal to make weapons and tools.

Coal Industry

The modern coal industry began during the **Industrial Revolution**. Before that time, coal was used mainly to heat homes and businesses.

In the early 1900s, trains used coal-burning steam engines to help people travel across the country.

In the late 1700s, James Watt invented a steam engine that burned coal. As this new technology caught on, the demand for coal grew. By the 1800s, coal-burning steamboats and trains traveled across the United States.

▲ Edwin L. Drake (right) and an engineer stand in front of the oil well Drake drilled in Titusville, Pennsylvania, in 1859.

FACT!

Today, the United States produces half of the oil it needs. The United States buys the rest of its oil from other countries.

In the 1880s, Thomas Edison built the first electric power plant in New York City. His plant burned coal. Edison's idea spread. Power companies began selling electricity so people could light homes and businesses.

Petroleum Industry

Edwin L. Drake started the U.S. oil industry in 1859. He drilled the country's first commercial oil well in Titusville, Pennsylvania. Many people called the well Drake's Folly. They thought he was making a big mistake. Few people knew what could be done with the petroleum.

▲ A woman pumps gasoline at a Massachusetts service station in 1937.

Soon, scientists found uses for petroleum. They could turn it into **kerosene** and gasoline. Kerosene became the main fuel for lighting homes. It was much better than candles or whale-oil lamps. Gasoline became popular as people began owning automobiles. Oil wells were drilled in Europe, South America, and the Middle East to supply gas for automobiles.

Natural Gas Industry

The natural gas industry also began in the 1800s. In 1821, William Hart dug the first natural gas well in Fredonia, New York. The Fredonia Gaslight and Water Works Company became the country's first natural gas company in 1858.

People used natural gas in many ways. Gas lamps lit city streets. People also began using natural gas for heating and cooking.

In 1935, lamplighters still lit gas lamps at Finsbury Park in London.
➡

In the 1900s, the natural gas industry continued to grow. In the 1920s, utility companies began building long-distance pipelines. In 1931, natural gas was piped from Texas to Chicago. Today, natural gas is piped all over the United States.

In 1944, workers buried a long-distance gas pipeline in Texas. The pipeline ▼ stretched 1,265 miles (2,036 kilometers).

Chapter 4

The Path to Power

Fossil fuels pass through many steps to make power. Coal is mined. Oil and natural gas are drilled. Oil and natural gas are **refined** to make other fuels and goods. Power plants burn coal, oil, and natural gas to make electricity.

Mining Coal

Mine workers use surface mining to reach coal beds close to Earth's surface. Large machines scrape away the top layers of dirt and rock. The coal is then blasted loose. Other machines load it onto trucks or railroad cars. Surface mines produce more than two-thirds of the coal in the United States.

Coal is blasted loose at a surface mine near Wright, Wyoming.

Underground mining reaches deep coal beds. Miners dig a tunnel straight down into the ground. They then use machines to dig side tunnels to reach the coal. The coal is lifted to the surface in small coal cars or on moving tracks.

An oil drill spins quickly as it drills a well hole into ▼ the ground.

Oil and Natural Gas

Oil and natural gas are drilled on land and at sea. Oil drillers use strong drill bits to get through rock. A liquid called drilling mud is pumped into the hole to cool the bit. The mud also moves rock and dirt up and out of the well hole. When oil or gas is reached, machines pump it into storage tanks or pipelines.

Making Energy

After they are drilled, oil and natural gas are sent to refineries. There, oil is heated to separate it into useful products. Natural gas is cleaned so it can be burned in furnaces and stoves.

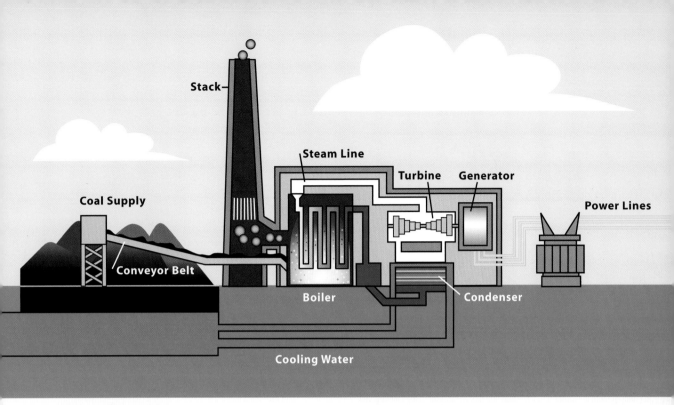

Stack

Steam Line

Turbine Generator

Coal Supply

Power Lines

Conveyor Belt

Boiler

Condenser

Cooling Water

▲ Coal-fired power plants burn large amounts of coal to make electricity.

Power plants burn coal, oil, and natural gas to make electricity. The burning fuel boils water. The water runs through hundreds of pipes inside the boiler. The boiling water turns into steam. The steam spins a **turbine**. As the turbine spins, it runs a **generator** that makes electricity.

After it leaves the turbine, the steam is changed back into water in a **condenser**. The water is then pumped back into the boiler.

19

Chapter 5

Benefits and Drawbacks

Fossil fuels provide the United States with more than 80 percent of its energy. About 40 percent of U.S. energy comes from oil. Like all kinds of energy, fossil fuels have benefits and drawbacks.

Benefits of Fossil Fuels

Fossil fuels have many good qualities. They make a large amount of energy from a small amount of fuel. They are found throughout the world. Fossil fuels are easy to store and move. They are also fairly cheap to mine and burn.

The Trans-Alaskan Pipeline carries crude oil from the Arctic Circle to Valdez, Alaska.

The oil tanker *Exxon Valdez* ran aground in Alaska on March 24, 1989. About 11 million gallons (42 million liters) of oil spilled into the ocean. About 200 miles (320 kilometers) of shoreline were damaged.

Smog hangs in the air above Los Angeles. Burning fossil fuels releases pollutants that ▼ can cause smog.

Fossil Fuel Drawbacks

Pollution is the biggest drawback to burning fossil fuels. Some chemicals from burned fuels pollute the air. Healthy people may find it hard to exercise or play outdoors in polluted air. People with asthma and other lung problems find it hard to breathe polluted air.

Burning coal makes sulfur dioxide. This colorless gas mixes with water vapor in the air to make acid rain. Acid rain can harm plants and animals.

▲ Steam rises
from an oil
refinery in
Joliet, Illinois.

All fossil fuels give off carbon dioxide when they burn. Most scientists agree that carbon dioxide plays a part in global warming. They believe this gas traps heat on Earth. The trapped heat can cause climate changes. A warmer climate could cause more storms and more tropical diseases. A warmer climate could also kill many types of plants and animals.

Chapter 6

The Future

Coal, petroleum, and natural gas are not renewable resources. People use them faster than nature can make them. One day the world will run out of fossil fuels.

Some scientists believe the United States has enough coal to last 250 years. They think the country has enough natural gas to last about 100 years. Many scientists think the world has enough oil to last only about 60 to 90 years. The demand for oil may be the world's biggest energy challenge in the coming years.

An offshore oil platform burns off natural gas while it drills oil.

FACT!

Scientists can change some waste into oil. With heat and pressure, it takes only a few minutes. A turkey processing plant in Carthage, Missouri, uses the process. They turn turkey skin, blood, and bones into oil. The oil can be used as fuel.

Looking Forward

People are always looking for other energy sources. Some companies are building wind farms to make electricity. Other companies are using wood or farm waste as fuel for power plants.

The Tracy Biomass Plant in Tracy, California, burns wood waste to make electricity.

Energy from fossil fuels touches our lives every day. Coal creates electricity to light our schools. Oil is made into gasoline to keep our cars running. Natural gas heats our homes and helps us cook our food. Fossil fuels supply us with most of the energy we use day and night. They will continue to be an important source of energy in the future.

Fast Facts

- Coal, oil, and natural gas are the three types of fossil fuels.

- About 25 percent of the world's coal is located in the United States.

- Edwin L. Drake started the U.S. oil industry in 1859. He drilled the country's first commercial oil well in Titusville, Pennsylvania.

- In 1858, the Fredonia Gaslight and Water Works Company became the first U.S. natural gas company.

- Raw natural gas is odorless. A chemical is added to the natural gas to make it smell like rotten eggs.

- Some power plants burn fossil fuels to create electricity.

- Coal, petroleum, and natural gas are not renewable resources. People use them faster than nature can create them.

- The United States buys half of the oil it needs from other countries.

Hands On: Distilling Water

Oil refineries distill crude oil to make useful fuel products. During distilling, oil is boiled. It is separated into gasoline, kerosene, motor oil, and other valuable petroleum products. A simple experiment with salt water shows how distillation works. Ask an adult to help you with this experiment.

What You Need

2 cups (480 mL) water

¼ cup (60 mL) salt

saucepan

wooden mixing spoon

stove

oversized saucepan lid

bowl

adult to help

What You Do

1. Pour water and salt into the saucepan. Stir with the mixing spoon until the salt can no longer be seen. Place the pan on a stove burner.
2. Place the oversized lid on the pan. Do not center the lid over the pan. Instead, allow one side of the lid to stick out.
3. Place bowl under the part of the lid that is sticking out. Make sure the bowl does not touch the burner.
4. Ask an adult to turn on heat and bring salt water to a boil.
5. Boil water for 5 minutes. Watch for water droplets to fall from the lid into the bowl.
6. Turn off heat. Let the water cool for 1 hour.
7. Taste the water in the saucepan.
8. Taste the water in the bowl.

How do they taste different? What came out of the water that fell into the bowl during distillation?

Index

Hands On: Distilling Water

Oil refineries distill crude oil to make useful fuel products. During distilling, oil is boiled. It is separated into gasoline, kerosene, motor oil, and other valuable petroleum products. A simple experiment with salt water shows how distillation works. Ask an adult to help you with this experiment.

What You Need
2 cups (480 mL) water   stove
¼ cup (60 mL) salt   oversized saucepan lid
saucepan   bowl
wooden mixing spoon   adult to help

What You Do
1. Pour water and salt into the saucepan. Stir with the mixing spoon until the salt can no longer be seen. Place the pan on a stove burner.
2. Place the oversized lid on the pan. Do not center the lid over the pan. Instead, allow one side of the lid to stick out.
3. Place bowl under the part of the lid that is sticking out. Make sure the bowl does not touch the burner.
4. Ask an adult to turn on heat and bring salt water to a boil.
5. Boil water for 5 minutes. Watch for water droplets to fall from the lid into the bowl.
6. Turn off heat. Let the water cool for 1 hour.
7. Taste the water in the saucepan.
8. Taste the water in the bowl.

How do they taste different? What came out of the water that fell into the bowl during distillation?

Glossary

condenser (kuhn-DENSS-ur)—a tank that changes steam into water

fossil (FOSS-uhl)—plant or animal remains preserved in rock

generator (JEN-uh-ray-tur)—a machine used to make electricity

Industrial Revolution (in-DUHSS-tree-uhl rev-uh-LOO-shuhn)—a period between 1790 and 1860 when the economy relied less on agriculture and more on factories and industry

kerosene (KER-uh-seen)—a thin, colorless fuel that is made from petroleum

pollution (puh-LOO-shuhn)—harmful materials that damage the environment

refine (ri-FINE)—to clean and make raw materials into finished products

turbine (TUR-buhn)—an engine powered by water, steam, or gas moving through the blades of a fan

Internet Sites

FactHound offers a safe, fun way to find Internet sites related to this book. All of the sites on FactHound have been researched by our staff.

Here's how:

1. Visit *www.facthound.com*
2. Type in this special code **0736824707** for age-appropriate sites. Or enter a search word related to this book for a more general search.
3. Click on the Fetch It button.

FactHound will fetch the best sites for you!

Read More

Dalgleish, Sharon. *Renewing Energy.* Our World. Philadelphia: Chelsea House, 2003.

Miller, Kimberly M. *What If We Run Out of Fossil Fuels?* High Interest Books. New York: Children's Press, 2002.

Oxlade, Chris. *How We Use Oil.* Using Materials. Chicago: Raintree, 2004.

Snedden, Robert. *Energy from Fossil Fuels.* Essential Energy. Chicago: Heinemann Library, 2002.

Index

coal, 4, 5, 6–7, 10–12,
16–17, 19, 22, 24, 27
mining, 6, 7, 16–17, 20

Drake, Edwin L., 12

Edison, Thomas, 12
electricity, 4, 6, 9, 12, 16,
19, 26, 27
Exxon Valdez, 22

Fredonia Gaslight and
Water Works
Company, 14

gas lamps, 14
gasoline, 8, 13, 27
global warming, 23

Hart, William, 14

Industrial Revolution, 10

natural gas, 6, 9, 10, 14–15,
16, 18, 19, 24, 25, 27
drilling, 9, 16, 18
refining, 16, 18

oil, 6, 8, 9, 10, 12–13, 16,
18, 19, 20, 21, 22, 23, 24,
25, 26, 27
drilling, 8, 12, 13, 16, 18
refining, 16, 18, 23

petroleum. See oil
pipelines, 15, 18, 21
pollution, 9, 22–23
power plant, 4, 5, 12, 16,
19, 26

steam engine, 11

Trans-Alaskan Pipeline, 21

Watt, James, 11

32